Shakespeare's Verse

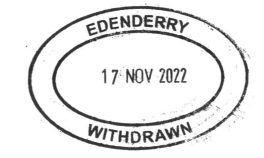

KINGFISHER
An imprint of Kingfisher Publications Plc
New Penderel House, 283-288 High Holborn
London WC1V 7HZ
www.kingfisherpub.com

First published in hardback by Kingfisher 1995
as *Something Rich and Strange: A Treasury of Shakespeare's Verse*
First published in paperback by Kingfisher 1998
This edition published by Kingfisher 2005
2 4 6 8 10 9 7 5 3 1

A CIP catalogue record for this book
is available from the British Library.

ISBN-13: 978 0 7534 1188 9
ISBN-10: 0 7534 1188 1

Printed in China
1TR/WKT/PW(MA)/128MA/F

Shakespeare's Verse

SELECTED BY
GINA
POLLINGER

ILLUSTRATED BY
EMMA
CHICHESTER CLARK

KINGFISHER

"Poetry has the same effect on words as wet sand on pennies. In what seems almost a miraculous way, it brightens up words that looked dull and ordinary...

"Don't let the playground bullies tell you that poetry is soft... a good poem is just about as hard as a diamond... think of the things you know that have the longest lives — yew trees, tortoises, marble temples, ancient castles. Well, a good poem can live on for centuries longer than a tortoise or a yew tree."
C. Day-Lewis *Poetry for You* (Basil Blackwell, 1944)

✦ CONTENTS ✦

✦ INTRODUCTION ✦

A Kingfisher Treasury of Shakespeare's Verse is directed, purely and simply, at those who read for pleasure. Those encountering Shakespeare's sixteenth-century language for the first time can take comfort from the words of the eighteenth-century critic, Dr Johnson, who observed that Shakespeare's creations "act and speak as the reader thinks he himself should have spoken or acted on the same occasion. . . the dialogue is level with life." Shakespeare, as actor and playwright, spent his entire working life burrowing under the skin of character, male and female, young and old, heroic and hapless, rustic and royal. He slips easily into all our shoes — even in the twenty-first century!

The imagery that links Shakespeare's powerful imagination to our own may be startling in colour, form and meaning but it draws upon objects that are universally familiar. These range from the homespun — such as milk, meat, drink, salad, slipper — to the world of nature — stars, moon, weed, lily, snail and so on. A perfect marriage of sound to sense ensures and enhances the effect:

"Then was I as a tree
Whose boughs did bend with fruit; but in one night
A storm or robbery, call it what you will,
Shook down my mellow hangings, nay, my leaves,
And left me bare to weather."

Cymbeline, Act III Scene iii

Such underlying simplicity demonstrates that Shakespeare's poetry and poetic drama were indeed written for all to enjoy, irrespective of social class and education.

This anthology is an orchestrated succession of relatively short clusters and sequences — all in the "rattling tongue of saucy and audacious eloquence" — linked in theme, extract to extract, section to section. The touchstone is immediacy, the keynote, almost always, passion: Shakespeare's verse was meant to be spoken, not read, and you will find the sense more obvious and the current of feeling twice as stirring, if you read aloud. Brief quotations act as headings at the top of each page — some merry, some sombre, some magic, some moody. My aim in including them was to smooth the flow and reinforce atmosphere, manner and direction. It may sound like a contradiction in terms but, from the first, I planned this anthology as a single composition, an overture that would pave the way and make access to Shakespeare that much easier.

In one sense, any anthology is likely to be unsatisfactory: something important must be missing! Since this is an anthology of Shakespeare's poetry — not Shakespeare's poetic drama — character and plot are the inevitable casualties. However, isolating the poetry does yield positive benefits. It concentrates the mind on the flexibility and range of Shakespeare's chosen medium, blank verse. It also demonstrates that Shakespeare's poetry enjoys a life of its own, regardless of dramatic context. When a besieged and bereaved

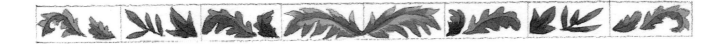

Macbeth surrenders to despair, the details of his personal tragedy become, for the moment, curiously unimportant:

> "Tomorrow, and tomorrow, and tomorrow
> Creeps in this petty pace from day to day,
> To the last syllable of recorded time,
> And all our yesterdays have lighted fools
> The way to dusty death. Out, out, brief candle.
> Life's but a walking shadow, a poor player
> That struts and frets his hour upon the stage,
> And then is heard no more. It is a tale
> Told by an idiot, full of sound and fury,
> Signifying nothing."
>
> *Macbeth, Act V Scene v*

The poetry speaks for itself and, in this particular case, for anyone who has — even for one moment — given up hope.

There are, of course, dark elements in this anthology, as there are in life itself, but good humour, sweet reason, beauty and reconciliation predominate. You have only to glance at the words of wit and wisdom strung across the pages to feel your spirits rise. For Shakespeare took neither himself nor his art too seriously. Here he is poking fun at poetry and playing to the crowd:

> "I had rather be a kitten and cry 'mew',
> Than one of these same metre ballad-mongers.
> I had rather hear a brazen canstick turned,
> Or a dry wheel grate on the axle-tree,
> And that would set my teeth nothing on edge,
> Nothing so much as mincing poetry.
> 'Tis like the forced gait of a shuffling nag."
>
> *Henry IV Part One, Act III Scene i*

Mincing poetry? Yes, Shakespeare was a master of self-mockery, too!

In this anthology, I have attempted to convey in miniature a faithful impression of the richness, gusto, intelligence and scope of Shakespeare's poetry. I hope the selection will prove more than a browser's delight: that some of you will be encouraged to look beyond it to even more spectacular discoveries — this time in the live theatre. For there you will hear this poetry — and much more, on themes now familiar — happily restored to character, plot and stage: Shakespeare in action, Shakespeare in the round, Shakespeare in all his glory.

GINA POLLINGER

For my mother
whose delight in all things beautiful
continues to inspire me.
G.P.

POWER TO CHARM

Come unto these yellow sands,
        And then take hands.

The Tempest, I ii

Be not afeard. The isle is full of noises,
Sounds, and sweet airs, that give delight and hurt not.
Sometimes a thousand twangling instruments
Will hum about mine ears, and sometime voices
That if I then had waked after long sleep
Will make me sleep again; and then in dreaming
The clouds methought would open and show riches
Ready to drop upon me, that when I waked
I cried to dream again.

The Tempest, III ii

Under the greenwood tree
   Who loves to lie with me,
   And turn his merry note
   Unto the sweet bird's throat,
Come hither, come hither, come hither.
   Here shall he see
   No enemy
But winter and rough weather.

   Who doth ambition shun,
   And loves to live i'th' sun,
   Seeking the food he eats
   And pleased with what he gets,
Come hither, come hither, come hither:
   Here shall he see
   No enemy
But winter and rough weather.
As You Like It, II v

And this our life, exempt from public haunt,
Finds tongues in trees, books in the running brooks,
Sermons in stones, and good in everything.
As You Like It, II i

Daffodils,
That come before the swallow dares, and take
The winds of March with beauty...
...pale primroses,
...bold oxlips,
...lilies of all kinds.
The Winter's Tale, IV iv

Hot lavender, mints, savory, marjoram,
The marigold, that goes to bed wi'th' sun,
And with him rises, weeping.
The Winter's Tale, IV iv

And winking Mary-buds begin
    to ope their golden eyes;
With everything that pretty is,
    my lady sweet, arise,
Arise, arise!
Cymbeline, II iii

Merrily, merrily
    shall I live now
Under the blossom that
    hangs on the bough.
The Tempest, V i

I know a bank where the wild thyme blows,
Where oxlips and the nodding violet grows,
Quite overcanopied with luscious woodbine,
With sweet musk-roses, and with eglantine.
There sleeps Titania sometime of the night,
Lulled in these flowers with dances and delight;
And there the snake throws her enamelled skin,
Weed wide enough to wrap a fairy in.

A Midsummer Night's Dream, II i

Where the bee sucks, there suck I:
In a cowslip's bell I lie;
There I couch when owls do cry.
On the bat's back I do fly.

The Tempest, V i

Over hill, over dale,
   Thorough bush, thorough brier,
Over park, over pale,
   Thorough flood, thorough fire:
I do wander everywhere
Swifter than the moonës sphere,
And I serve the Fairy Queen
To dew her orbs upon the green.
The cowslips tall her pensioners be.
In their gold coats spots you see;
Those be rubies, fairy favours;
In those freckles live their savours.
I must go seek some dewdrops here,
And hang a pearl in every cowslip's ear.

A Midsummer Night's Dream, II i

You spotted snakes with double tongue,
  Thorny hedgehogs, be not seen;
Newts and blindworms, do no wrong;
  Come not near our Fairy Queen.

Weaving spiders, come not here;
  Hence, you long-legged spinners, hence;
Beetles black, approach not near;
  Worm nor snail do no offence.

  Philomel with melody,
  Sing in our sweet lullaby;
Lulla, lulla, lullaby; lulla, lulla, lullaby.
    Never harm,
    Nor spell nor charm
  Come our lovely lady nigh.
  So good night, with lullaby.
A Midsummer Night's Dream, II ii

She bids you on the wanton rushes lay you down
And rest your gentle head upon her lap,
And she will sing the song that pleaseth you
And on your eyelids crown the god of sleep,
Charming your blood with pleasing heaviness.
1 Henry IV, III i

Peaseblossom, Cobweb, Mote, and Mustardseed!
Be kind and courteous to this gentleman.
Hop in his walks, and gambol in his eyes.
Feed him with apricots and dewberries,
With purple grapes, green figs, and mulberries;
The honeybags steal from the humble-bees,
And for night tapers crop their waxen thighs
And light them at the fiery glow-worms' eyes
To have my love to bed, and to arise;
And pluck the wings from painted butterflies
To fan the moonbeams from his sleeping eyes.
Nod to him, elves, and do him courtesies.

A Midsummer Night's Dream, III i

Through the house give glimmering light.
  By the dead and drowsy fire
Every elf and fairy sprite
  Hop as light as bird from brier,
And this ditty after me
Sing, and dance it trippingly.

First rehearse your song by rote,
To each word a warbling note.
Hand in hand with fairy grace
Will we sing and bless this place.

A Midsummer Night's Dream, V ii

Light thickens, and the crow
Makes wing to th' rooky wood.
Good things of day begin to droop and drowse,
Whiles night's black agents to their preys do rouse.
Macbeth, III ii

'Tis now the very witching time of night,
When churchyards yawn, and hell itself
   breathes out
Contagion to this world.

Hamlet, III ii

The time has been
That, when the brains were out, the man would die,
And there an end. But now they rise again
With twenty mortal murders on their crowns,
And push us from our stools.

Macbeth, III iv

In the most high and palmy state of Rome,
A little ere the mightiest Julius fell,
The graves stood tenantless, and the sheeted dead
Did squeak and gibber in the Roman streets.

Hamlet, I i

Now o'er the one half-world
Nature seems dead, and wicked dreams abuse
The curtained sleep. Witchcraft celebrates
Pale Hecate's offerings, and withered murder,
Alarumed by his sentinel the wolf,
Whose howl's his watch, thus with his stealthy pace,
With Tarquin's ravishing strides, towards his design
Moves like a ghost.

Macbeth, II i

What are these
So withered, and so wild in their attire,
That look not like th'inhabitants o'th'earth,
And yet are on't?

Macbeth, I iii

FIRST WITCH
When shall we three meet again?
In thunder, lightning, or in rain?
SECOND WITCH
When the hurly-burly's done,
When the battle's lost and won.
THIRD WITCH
That will be ere the set of sun.
FIRST WITCH
Where the place?
SECOND WITCH
            Upon the heath.
THIRD WITCH
There to meet with Macbeth.
FIRST WITCH
I come, Grimalkin.
SECOND WITCH
Paddock calls.
THIRD WITCH
          Anon.
ALL
Fair is foul, and foul is fair,
Hover through the fog and filthy air.
Macbeth, I i

FIRST WITCH

Round about the cauldron go,
In the poisoned entrails throw.
Toad that under cold stone
Days and nights has thirty-one
Sweltered venom sleeping got,
Boil thou first i'th' charmèd pot.

ALL

Double, double, toil and trouble,
Fire burn, and cauldron bubble.

SECOND WITCH

Fillet of a fenny snake,
In the cauldron boil and bake.
Eye of newt and toe of frog,
Wool of bat and tongue of dog,
Adder's fork and blind-worm's sting,
Lizard's leg and owlet's wing,
For a charm of powerful trouble,
Like a hell-broth boil and bubble.

ALL

Double, double, toil and trouble,
Fire burn, and cauldron bubble...

SECOND WITCH

By the pricking of my thumbs,
Something wicked this way comes.
Open, locks, whoever knocks.

MACBETH

How now, you secret, black, and midnight hags,
What is't you do?

ALL

A deed without a name.

Macbeth, IV i

The night has been unruly. Where we lay
Our chimneys were blown down, and, as they say,
Lamentings heard i'th' air, strange screams of death,
And prophesying with accents terrible
Of dire combustion and confused events
New-hatched to th' woeful time. The obscure bird
Clamoured the livelong night. Some say the earth
Was feverous and did shake.

Macbeth, II iii

             I have heard
The cock, that is the trumpet to the morn,
Doth with his lofty and shrill-sounding throat
Awake the god of day, and at his warning,
Whether in sea or fire, in earth or air,
Th'extravagant and erring spirit hies
To his confine.

Hamlet, I i

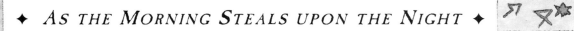

Good morrow, masters, put your torches out.
    The wolves have preyed, and look, the gentle day
Before the wheels of Phoebus round about
    Dapples the drowsy east with spots of grey.

Much Ado About Nothing, V iii

Lo, here the gentle lark, weary of rest,
From his moist cabinet mounts up on high
And wakes the morning, from whose silver breast
The sun ariseth in his majesty,
    Who doth the world so gloriously behold
    That cedar tops and hills seem burnished gold.

Venus and Adonis, ll. 853-858

Night's candles are burnt out, and jocund day
Stands tiptoe on the misty mountain tops.
Romeo and Juliet, III v

Even till the eastern gate, all fiery red,
Opening on Neptune with fair blessèd beams
Turns into yellow gold his salt green streams…
A Midsummer Night's Dream, III ii

Kissing with golden face the meadows green,
Gilding pale streams with heavenly alchemy.
Sonnet 33

YOUTH, I DO ADORE THEE!

Crabbèd age and youth
Cannot live together:
Youth is full of pleasance,
Age is full of care;
Youth like summer morn,
Age like winter weather;
Youth like summer brave,
Age like winter bare.
Youth is full of sport,
Age's breath is short.
Youth is nimble, Age is lame,
Youth is hot and bold,
Age is weak and cold.
Youth is wild, and Age is tame.
　　Age, I do abhor thee;
　　Youth, I do adore thee.
　　　　O my love, my love is young.
　　Age, I do defy thee.
　　　　O sweet shepherd, hie thee,
For methinks thou stay'st too long.
The Passionate Pilgrim, Pt 12

Behold, my lords,
Although the print be little, the whole matter
And copy of the father: eye, nose, lip,
The trick of's frown, his forehead, nay, the valley,
The pretty dimples of his chin and cheek, his smiles,
The very mould and frame of hand, nail, finger.

The Winter's Tale, II iii

But thou art fair, and at thy birth, dear boy,
Nature and Fortune joined to make thee great.
Of Nature's gifts thou mayst with lilies boast,
And with the half-blown rose.

King John, II ii

Thou art thy mother's glass, and she in thee
Calls back the lovely April of her prime.

Sonnet 3

VALERIA
How does your little son?

VIRGILIA
I thank your ladyship; well, good madam.

VOLUMNIA
He had rather see the swords and hear a drum
than look upon his schoolmaster.

VALERIA
O' my word, the father's son!

Coriolanus, I iii

We were, fair Queen,
Two lads that thought there was no more behind
But such a day tomorrow as today,
And to be boy eternal.
The Winter's Tale, I ii

We were as twinned lambs that did frisk i'th' sun,
And bleat the one at th'other. What we changed
Was innocence for innocence. We knew not
The doctrine of ill-doing, no, nor dreamed
That any did. Had we pursued that life,
And our weak spirits ne'er been higher reared
With stronger blood, we should have answered heaven
Boldly, "Not guilty", the imposition cleared
Hereditary ours.
The Winter's Tale, I ii

I was too young that time to value her,
But now I know her. If she be a traitor,
Why, so am I. We still have slept together,
Rose at an instant, learned, played, eat together,
And wheresoe'er we went, like Juno's swans,
Still we went coupled and inseparable.

As You Like It, I iii

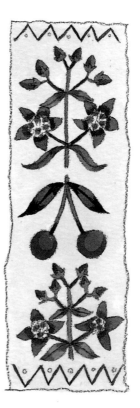

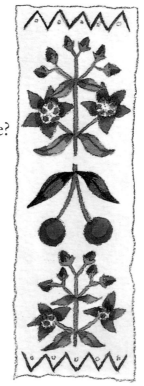

Is all the counsel that we two have shared —
The sisters' vows, the hours that we have spent
When we have chid the hasty-footed time
For parting us — O, is all quite forgot?
All schooldays' friendship, childhood innocence?
We, Hermia, like two artificial gods
Have with our needles created both one flower,
Both on one sampler, sitting on one cushion,
Both warbling of one song, both in one key,
As if our hands, our sides, voices, and minds
Had been incorporate. So we grew together,
Like to a double cherry: seeming parted,
But yet an union in partition,
Two lovely berries moulded on one stem.

A Midsummer Night's Dream, III ii

Think not I love him, though I ask for him.
'Tis but a peevish boy. Yet he talks well.
But what care I for words? Yet words do well
When he that speaks them pleases those that hear.
It is a pretty youth — not very pretty —
But sure he's proud; and yet his pride becomes him.
He'll make a proper man. The best thing in him
Is his complexion; and faster than his tongue
Did make offence, his eye did heal it up.
He is not very tall; yet for his years he's tall.
His leg is but so-so; and yet 'tis well.
There was a pretty redness in his lip,
A little riper and more lusty red
Than that mixed in his cheek. 'Twas just the difference
Betwixt the constant red and mingled damask.

As You Like It, III v

My salad days,
When I was green in judgement.

Antony and Cleopatra, I v

Some say thy fault is youth, some wantonness.

Sonnet 96

The tongues of mocking wenches are as keen
  As is the razor's edge invisible,
Cutting a smaller hair than may be seen,
  Above the sense of sense; so sensible
Seemeth their conference. Their conceits have wings
Fleeter than arrows, bullets, wind, thought, swifter things.

Love's Labour's Lost, V ii

SILVIUS

O Corin, that thou knew'st how I do love her!

CORIN

I partly guess; for I have loved ere now.

SILVIUS

No, Corin, being old thou canst not guess,
Though in thy youth thou wast as true a lover
As ever sighed upon a midnight pillow.

As You Like It, II iv

What is love? 'Tis not hereafter,
Present mirth hath present laughter.
    What's to come is still unsure.
In delay there lies no plenty,
Then come kiss me, sweet and twenty.
    Youth's a stuff will not endure.

Twelfth Night, II iii

IT WAS A LOVER AND HIS LASS

It was a lover and his lass,
　　With a hey, and a ho, and a hey-nonny-no,
That o'er the green cornfield did pass
　　In spring-time, the only pretty ring-time,
When birds do sing, hey ding-a-ding ding,
Sweet lovers love the spring.

As You Like It, V iii

VALENTINE

Why, how know you that I am in love?

SPEED

Marry, by these special marks: first, you have learned, like Sir Proteus, to wreathe your arms, like a malcontent; to relish a love-song, like a robin redbreast; to walk alone, like one that had the pestilence; to sigh, like a schoolboy that had lost his ABC; to weep, like a young wench that had buried her grandam; to fast, like one that takes diet; to watch, like one that fears robbing; to speak puling, like a beggar at Hallowmas. You were wont, when you laughed, to crow like a cock; when you walked, to walk like one of the lions. When you fasted, it was presently after dinner; when you looked sadly, it was for want of money. And now you are metamorphosed with a mistress, that when I look on you I can hardly think you my master.

The Two Gentlemen of Verona, II i

He does smile his face into more lines than is in the new map with the augmentation of the Indies. You have not seen such a thing as 'tis. I can hardly forbear hurling things at him.

Twelfth Night, III ii

Proceed, sweet Cupid, thou hast thumped him
with thy birdbolt under the left pap.
Love's Labour's Lost, IV iii

I have known when there was no music with
him but the drum and the fife, and now had he
rather hear the tabor and the pipe. I have known
when he would have walked ten mile afoot to see
a good armour, and now will he lie ten nights
awake carving the fashion of a new doublet. He
was wont to speak plain and to the purpose, like
an honest man and a soldier, and now is he turned
orthography. His words are a very fantastical
banquet, just so many strange dishes.
Much Ado About Nothing, II iii

If thou rememberest not the slightest folly
That ever love did make thee run into,
Thou hast not loved.
As You Like It, II iv

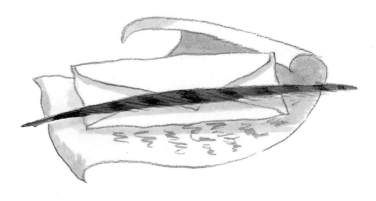

O coz, coz, coz, my pretty little coz, that thou didst know how many fathom deep I am in love. But it cannot be sounded. My affection hath an unknown bottom, like the Bay of Portugal.

As You Like It, IV i

He says he loves my daughter.
I think so, too, for never gazed the moon
Upon the water as he'll stand and read,
As 'twere, my daughter's eyes; and to be plain,
I think there is not half a kiss to choose
Who loves another best.

The Winter's Tale, IV iv

Tell me where is fancy bred,
Or in the heart, or in the head?
How begot, how nourishèd?
  Reply, reply.
It is engendered in the eyes,
With gazing fed.

The Merchant of Venice, III ii

A lover's eyes will gaze an eagle blind.
A lover's ear will hear the lowest sound.

Love's Labour's Lost, IV iii

Her lily hand her rosy cheek lies under,
Coz'ning the pillow of a lawful kiss.
The Rape of Lucrece, ll. 386-387

O, she doth teach the torches to burn bright!
It seems she hangs upon the cheek of night
As a rich jewel in an Ethiope's ear.
Romeo and Juliet, I v

O happy fair!
Your eyes are lodestars, and your tongue's sweet air
More tuneable than lark to shepherd's ear
When wheat is green, when hawthorn buds appear.
A Midsummer Night's Dream, I i

Her voice was ever soft,
Gentle, and low, an excellent thing in woman.
King Lear, V iii

In love — ay, faith, to the very tip of the nose.
Troilus and Cressida, III i

JACQUES
What stature is she of?
ORLANDO
Just as high as my heart.
As You Like It, III ii

I will tell you.
The barge she sat in, like a burnished throne
Burned on the water. The poop was beaten gold;
Purple the sails, and so perfumèd that
The winds were love-sick with them. The oars were silver,
Which to the tune of flutes kept stroke, and made
The water which they beat to follow faster,
As amorous of their strokes. For her own person,
It beggared all description. She did lie
In her pavilion — cloth of gold, of tissue —
O'er-picturing that Venus where we see
The fancy outwork nature. On each side her
Stood pretty dimpled boys, like smiling Cupids,
With divers-coloured fans whose wind did seem
To glow the delicate cheeks which they did cool,
And what they undid did.

Antony and Cleopatra, II ii

Age cannot wither her, nor custom stale
Her infinite variety. Other women cloy
The appetites they feed, but she makes hungry
Where most she satisfies.

Antony and Cleopatra, II ii

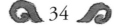

His legs bestrid the ocean; his reared arm
Crested the world. His voice was propertied
As all the tunèd spheres, and that to friends;
But when he meant to quail and shake the orb,
He was as rattling thunder. For his bounty,
There was no winter in't; an autumn 'twas,
That grew the more by reaping. His delights
Were dolphin-like; they showed his back above
The element they lived in. In his livery
Walked crowns and crownets. Realms and islands were
As plates dropped from his pocket.

Antony and Cleopatra, V ii

DROMIO OF SYRACUSE

I am an ass, I am a woman's man, and besides myself.

ANTIPHOLUS OF SYRACUSE

What woman's man? And how besides thyself?

DROMIO OF SYRACUSE

Marry, sir, besides myself I am due to a woman: one that
claims me, one that haunts me, one that will have me...
I have but lean luck in the match, and yet is she a
wondrous fat marriage.

ANTIPHOLUS OF SYRACUSE

How dost thou mean, a fat marriage?

DROMIO OF SYRACUSE

Marry, sir, she's the kitchen wench, and all grease; and I
know not what use to put her to but to make a lamp of her,
and run from her by her own light. I warrant her rags and
the tallow in them will burn a Poland winter. If she lives till
doomsday, she'll burn a week longer than the whole world.

The Comedy of Errors, III ii

LORENZO

The moon shines bright. . . In such a night
Troilus, methinks, mounted the Trojan walls,
And sighed his soul toward the Grecian tents
Where Cressid lay that night.

JESSICA

          In such a night
Did Thisbe fearfully o'ertrip the dew
And saw the lion's shadow ere himself,
And ran dismayed away.

LORENZO

          In such a night
Stood Dido with a willow in her hand
Upon the wild sea banks, and waft her love
To come again to Carthage.

JESSICA

          In such a night
Medea gatherèd the enchanted herbs
That did renew old Aeson.

LORENZO

          In such a night
Did Jessica steal from the wealthy Jew,
And with an unthrift love did run from Venice
As far as Belmont.

JESSICA

          In such a night
Did young Lorenzo swear he loved her well,
Stealing her soul with many vows of faith,
And ne'er a true one.

LORENZO

          In such a night
Did pretty Jessica, like a little shrew,
Slander her love, and he forgave it her.

The Merchant of Venice, V i

When you speak, sweet,
I'd have you do it ever; when you sing,
I'd have you buy and sell so, so give alms,
Pray so; and for the ord'ring your affairs,
To sing them too. When you do dance, I wish you
A wave o'th' sea, that you might ever do
Nothing but that, move still, still so,
And own no other function. Each your doing,
So singular in each particular,
Crowns what you are doing in the present deeds,
That all your acts are queens.

The Winter's Tale, IV iv

ORSINO

How dost thou like this tune?

VIOLA

It gives a very echo to the seat
Where love is throned.

Twelfth Night, II iv

If music be the food of love, play on,
Give me excess of it that, surfeiting,
The appetite may sicken and so die.
That strain again, it had a dying fall.
O, it came o'er my ear like the sweet sound
That breathes upon a bank of violets,
Stealing and giving odour. Enough, no more,
'Tis not so sweet now as it was before.

Twelfth Night, I i

Music, moody food of us that trade in love.

Antony and Cleopatra, II v

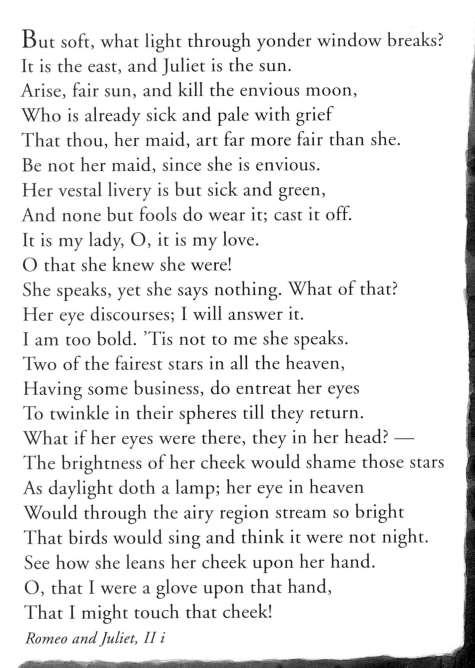

But soft, what light through yonder window breaks?
It is the east, and Juliet is the sun.
Arise, fair sun, and kill the envious moon,
Who is already sick and pale with grief
That thou, her maid, art far more fair than she.
Be not her maid, since she is envious.
Her vestal livery is but sick and green,
And none but fools do wear it; cast it off.
It is my lady, O, it is my love.
O that she knew she were!
She speaks, yet she says nothing. What of that?
Her eye discourses; I will answer it.
I am too bold. 'Tis not to me she speaks.
Two of the fairest stars in all the heaven,
Having some business, do entreat her eyes
To twinkle in their spheres till they return.
What if her eyes were there, they in her head? —
The brightness of her cheek would shame those stars
As daylight doth a lamp; her eye in heaven
Would through the airy region stream so bright
That birds would sing and think it were not night.
See how she leans her cheek upon her hand.
O, that I were a glove upon that hand,
That I might touch that cheek!

Romeo and Juliet, II i

Love's feeling is more soft and sensible
Than are the tender horns of cockled snails.
Love's Labour's Lost, IV iii

Or as the snail, whose tender horns being hit
Shrinks backward in his shelly cave with pain,
And there, all smothered up, in shade doth sit,
Long after fearing to creep forth again.
Venus and Adonis, ll. 1033-1036

That I might sleep out this great gap of time
My Antony is away.
Antony and Cleopatra, I v

From you have I been absent in the spring
When proud-pied April, dressed in all his trim,
Hath put a spirit of youth in everything,
That heavy Saturn laughed and leapt with him.
Yet nor the lays of birds nor the sweet smell
Of different flowers in odour and in hue
Could make me any summer's story tell,
Or from their proud lap pluck them where they
    grew;
Nor did I wonder at the lily's white,
Nor praise the deep vermilion in the rose.
They were but sweet, but figures of delight
Drawn after you, you pattern of all those;
    Yet seemed it winter still, and, you away,
    As with your shadow I with these did play.
Sonnet 98

Except I be by Silvia in the night
There is no music in the nightingale.
Unless I look on Silvia in the day
There is no day for me to look upon.
The Two Gentlemen of Verona, III i

Being your slave, what should I do but tend
Upon the hours and times of your desire?
I have no precious time at all to spend,
Nor services to do, till you require;
Nor dare I chide the world-without-end hour
Whilst I, my sovereign, watch the clock for you,
Nor think the bitterness of absence sour
When you have bid your servant once adieu.
Nor dare I question with my jealous thought
Where you may be, or your affairs suppose,
But like a sad slave stay and think of naught
Save, where you are, how happy you make those.
   So true a fool is love that in your will,
   Though you do anything, he thinks no ill.

Sonnet 57

The course of true love never did run smooth.

A Midsummer Night's Dream, I i

So holy and so perfect is my love,
And I in such a poverty of grace,
That I shall think it a most plenteous crop
To glean the broken ears after the man
That the main harvest reaps. Loose now and then
A scattered smile, and that I'll live upon.

As You Like It, III v

Let me not to the marriage of true minds
Admit impediments. Love is not love
Which alters when it alteration finds,
Or bends with the remover to remove.
O no, it is an ever fixèd mark,
That looks on tempests, and is never shaken;
It is the star to every wand'ring barque,
Whose worth's unknown although his height be taken.
Love's not time's fool, though rosy lips and cheeks
Within his bending sickle's compass come;
Love alters not with his brief hours and weeks,
But bears it out even to the edge of doom.
    If this be error and upon me proved,
      I never writ, nor no man ever loved.

Sonnet 116

Hang there like fruit, my soul,
Till the tree die.

Cymbeline, V vi

 # THE ENVIOUS COURT

Who loses and who wins, who's in, who's out.
King Lear, V iii

The art o'th' court,
As hard to leave as keep, whose top to climb
Is certain falling, or so slipp'ry that
The fear's as bad as falling.
Cymbeline, III iii

If God have lent a man any manners he may easily put it off at court. He that cannot make a leg, put off's cap, kiss his hand, and say nothing, has neither leg, hands, lip nor cap, and indeed such a fellow, to say precisely, were not for the court.
All's Well That Ends Well, II ii

A certain lord, neat and trimly dressed,
Fresh as a bridegroom, and his chin, new-reaped,
Showed like a stubble-land at harvest-home.
He was perfumèd like a milliner,
And 'twixt his finger and his thumb he held
A pouncet-box, which ever and anon
He gave his nose and took't away again.
1 Henry IV, I iii

Those that are good manners at the court are as ridiculous in the country as the behaviour of the country is most mockable at the court. You told me you salute not at the court but you kiss your hands. That courtesy would be uncleanly if courtiers were shepherds. . . The courtier's hands are perfumed with civet.
As You Like It, III ii

This fellow pecks up wit as pigeons peas,
And utters it again when God doth please.
He is wit's pedlar, and retails his wares
At wakes and wassails, meetings, markets, fairs...
This gallant pins the wenches on his sleeve.
Had he been Adam, he had tempted Eve...
This is the ape of form, Monsieur Le Nice,
That when he plays at tables chides the dice
In honourable terms. Nay, he can sing
A mean most meanly, and in ushering
Mend him who can. The ladies call him sweet.
The stairs as he treads on them kiss his feet.

Love's Labour's Lost, V ii

Taffeta phrases, silken terms precise,
Three-piled hyperboles, spruce affectation,
Figures pedantical...

Love's Labour's Lost, V ii

These fellows of infinite tongue, that can rhyme themselves
into ladies' favours, they do always reason themselves out again.

Henry V, V ii

A courtier... could say, "Good morrow, sweet lord. How dost thou, good lord?" This might be my lord such a one, that praised my lord such a one's horse when a meant to beg it.

Hamlet, V i

Not a courtier —
Although they wear their faces to the bent
Of the King's looks — hath a heart that is not
Glad of the thing they scowl at.

Cymbeline, I i

There's no art
To find the mind's construction in the face.

Macbeth, I iv

When I tell him he hates flatterers;
He says he does, being then most flattered.

Julius Caesar, II i

THE KING IS BUT A MAN

Some are born great, some achieve greatness,
and some have greatness thrust upon 'em.
Twelfth Night, II v

Not all the water in the rough rude sea
Can wash the balm from an anointed king.
The breath of worldly men cannot depose
The deputy elected by the Lord.
Richard II, III ii

I think the King is but a man, as I am.
The violet smells to him as it doth to me;
the element shows to him as it doth to me.
All his senses have but human conditions.
His ceremonies laid by, in his nakedness he
appears but a man, and though his affections
are higher mounted than ours, yet when they
stoop, they stoop with the like wing.
Henry V, IV i

How many thousand of my poorest subjects
Are at this hour asleep? O sleep, O gentle sleep,
Nature's soft nurse, how have I frighted thee,
That thou no more wilt weigh my eyelids down
And steep my senses in forgetfulness?
Why rather, sleep, liest thou in smoky cribs,
Upon uneasy pallets stretching thee,
And hushed with buzzing night-flies to thy slumber,
Than in the perfumed chambers of the great,
Under the canopies of costly state,
And lulled with sound of sweetest melody?
O thou dull god, why li'st thou with the vile
In loathsome beds, and leav'st the kingly couch
A watch-case, or a common 'larum-bell?
Wilt thou upon the high and giddy mast
Seal up the ship-boy's eyes, and rock his brains
In cradle of the rude imperious surge,
And in the visitation of the winds,
Who take the ruffian billows by the top,
Curling their monstrous heads, and hanging them
With deafing clamour in the slippery clouds,
That, with the hurly, death itself awakes?
Canst thou, O partial sleep, give thy repose
To the wet sea-boy in an hour so rude,
And in the calmest and most stillest night,
With all appliances and means to boot,
Deny it to a king? Then happy low, lie down.
Uneasy lies the head that wears a crown.
2 Henry IV, III i

I swear, 'tis better to be lowly born
And range with humble livers in content
Than to be perked up in a glist'ring grief
And wear a golden sorrow.
Henry VIII, II iii

Ah, what a life were this! How sweet! How lovely!
Gives not the hawthorn bush a sweeter shade
To shepherds looking on their seely sheep
Than doth a rich embroidered canopy
To kings that fear their subjects' treachery?
3 Henry VI, II v

To be, or not to be; that is the question:
Whether 'tis nobler in the mind to suffer
The slings and arrows of outrageous fortune,
Or to take arms against a sea of troubles,
And, by opposing, end them. To die, to sleep —
No more, and by a sleep to say we end
The heartache and the thousand natural shocks
That flesh is heir to — 'tis a consummation
Devoutly to be wished. To die, to sleep.
To sleep, perchance to dream. Ay, there's the rub,
For in that sleep of death what dreams may come
When we have shuffled off this mortal coil
Must give us pause. There's the respect
That makes calamity of so long life,
For who would bear the whips and scorns of time,
Th'oppressor's wrong, the proud man's contumely,
The pangs of disprized love, the law's delay,
The insolence of office, and the spurns
That patient merit of th'unworthy takes,
When he himself might his quietus make
With a bare bodkin? Who would these fardels bear,
To grunt and sweat under a weary life,
But that the dread of something after death,
The undiscovered country from whose bourn
No traveller returns, puzzles the will,
And makes us rather bear those ills we have
Than fly to others that we know not of?
Thus conscience does make cowards of us all.
Hamlet, III i

O God, I could be bounded in a nutshell and count myself a king of infinite space, were it not that I have bad dreams.

Hamlet, II ii

O I have passed a miserable night,
So full of fearful dreams, of ugly sights,
That as I am a Christian faithful man,
I would not spend another such a night
Though 'twere to buy a world of happy days,
So full of dismal terror was the time.

Richard III, I iv

O Lord! Methought what pain it was to drown,
What dreadful noise of waters in my ears,
What sights of ugly death within my eyes.
Methoughts I saw a thousand fearful wrecks,
Ten thousand men that fishes gnawed upon,
Wedges of gold, great ouches, heaps of pearl,
Inestimable stones, unvalued jewels,
All scattered in the bottom of the sea.
Some lay in dead men's skulls; and in those holes
Where eyes did once inhabit, there were crept —
As 'twere in scorn of eyes — reflecting gems,
Which wooed the slimy bottom of the deep
And mocked the dead bones that lay scattered by.

Richard III, I iv

There is nothing either good or bad but thinking makes it so.
Hamlet, II ii

O that this too too solid flesh would melt,
Thaw, and resolve itself into a dew,
Or that the Everlasting had not fixed
His canon 'gainst self-slaughter! O God, O God,
How weary, stale, flat, and unprofitable
Seem to me all the uses of this world!
Fie on't, ah fie, fie! 'Tis an unweeded garden,
That grows to seed; things rank and gross in nature
Possess it merely.
Hamlet, I ii

Better be with the dead,
Whom we to gain our peace have sent to peace,
Than on the torture of the mind to lie
In restless ecstasy.
Macbeth, III ii

And I — like one lost in a thorny wood,
That rends the thorns and is rent with the thorns,
Seeking a way and straying from the way,
Not knowing how to find the open air,
But toiling desperately to find it out —
Torment myself to catch the English crown.
And from that torment I will free myself,
Or hew my way out with a bloody axe.
3 Henry VI, III ii

FIERCE CIVIL STRIFE

In cities, mutinies; in countries, discord; in palaces,
treason; and the bond cracked 'twixt son and father...
We have seen the best of our time. Machinations,
hollowness, treachery, and all ruinous disorders
follow us disquietly to our graves.

King Lear, I ii

And Liberty plucks Justice by the nose,
The baby beats the nurse, and quite athwart
Goes all decorum.

Measure for Measure, I iii

The children yet unborn
Shall feel this day as sharp to them as thorn.

Richard II, IV i

England now is left
To tug and scramble, and to part by th' teeth
The unowed interest of proud swelling state.
Now for the bare-picked bone of majesty
Doth doggèd war bristle his angry crest,
And snarleth in the gentle eyes of peace;
Now powers from home and discontents at home
Meet in one line, and vast confusion waits,
As doth a raven on a sick-fall'n beast,
The imminent decay of wrested pomp.
Now happy he whose cloak and cincture can
Hold out this tempest.

King John, IV iii

Blood and destruction shall be so in use,
And dreadful objects so familiar,
That mothers shall but smile when they behold
Their infants quartered with the hands of war.

Julius Caesar, III i

That England that was wont to conquer others
Hath made a shameful conquest of itself.

Richard II, II i

What must the King do now? Must he submit?
The King shall do it. Must he be deposed?
The King shall be contented. Must he lose
The name of King? A God's name, let it go.
I'll give my jewels for a set of beads,
My gorgeous palace for a hermitage,
My gay apparel for an almsman's gown,
My figured goblets for a dish of wood,
My sceptre for a palmer's walking staff,
My subjects for a pair of carvèd saints,
And my large kingdom for a little grave,
A little, little grave, an obscure grave;
Or I'll be buried in the King's highway,
Some way of common trade, where subjects' feet
May hourly trample on their sovereign's head,
For on my heart they tread now, whilst I live.

Richard II, III iii

 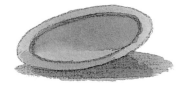

O, now for ever
Farewell the tranquil mind, farewell content,
Farewell the plumèd troops, and the big wars
That makes ambition virtue! O, farewell,
Farewell the neighing steed and the shrill trump,
The spirit-stirring drum, th'ear-piercing fife,
The royal banner, and all quality,
Pride, pomp, and circumstance of glorious war!
And O, you mortal engines whose rude throats
Th'immortal Jove's dread clamours counterfeit,
Farewell! Othello's occupation's gone!
Othello, III iii

Reputation, reputation, reputation — O, I ha' lost my reputation,
I ha' lost the immortal part of myself, and what remains is bestial!
Othello, II iii

I have lived long enough. My way of life
Is fall'n into the sere, the yellow leaf,
And that which should accompany old age,
As honour, love, obedience, troops of friends,
I must not look to have, but in their stead,
Curses, not loud but deep, mouth-honour, breath
Which the poor heart would fain deny and dare not.
Macbeth, V iii

O let not virtue seek
Remuneration for the thing it was;
For beauty, wit,
High birth, vigour of bone, desert in service,
Love, friendship, charity, are subjects all
To envious and calumniating time.
Troilus and Cressida, III iii

Here I stand your slave,
A poor, infirm, weak and despised old man.
King Lear, III ii

Thus are my blossoms blasted in the bud,
And caterpillars eat my leaves away.
2 Henry VI, III i

I have touched the highest point of all my greatness,
And from that full meridian of my glory
I haste now to my setting. I shall fall
Like a bright exhalation in the evening,
And no man see me more.

Henry VIII, III ii

Life's but a walking shadow, a poor player
That struts and frets his hour upon the stage,
And then is heard no more. It is a tale
Told by an idiot, full of sound and fury,
Signifying nothing.

Macbeth, V v

O mighty Caesar! Dost thou lie so low?
Are all thy conquests, glories, triumphs, spoils,
Shrunk to this little measure?

Julius Caesar, III i

But a clod
And module of confounded royalty.

King John, V vii

 # OUR LIFE IS OF A MINGLED YARN

They say best men are moulded out of faults,
And, for the most, become much more the better
For being a little bad.
Measure for Measure, V i

Virtue that transgresses is but patched with sin,
and sin that amends is but patched with virtue.
Twelfth Night, I v

Roses have thorns, and silver fountains mud.
Clouds and eclipses stain both moon and sun.
Sonnet 35

What a piece of work is a man! How noble in reason, how infinite in faculty, in form and moving how express and admirable, in action how like an angel, in apprehension how like a god — the beauty of the world, the paragon of animals! And yet to me what is this quintessence of dust?

Hamlet, II ii

'Tis in ourselves that we are thus or thus. Our bodies are our gardens, to the which our wills are gardeners; so that if we will plant nettles or sow lettuce, set hyssop and weed up thyme, supply it with one gender of herbs or distract it with many, either to have it sterile with idleness or manured with industry, why, the power and corrigible authority of this lies in our wills.

Othello, I iii

Why should the worm intrude the maiden bud,
Or hateful cuckoos hatch in sparrows' nests,
Or toads infect fair founts with venom mud,
Or tyrant folly lurk in gentle breasts,
Or kings be breakers of their own behests?
   But no perfection is so absolute
   That some impurity doth not pollute.

The Rape of Lucrece, ll. 848-854

If our virtues
Did not go forth of us, 'twere all alike
As if we had them not.
Measure for Measure, I i

My bounty is as boundless as the sea,
My love as deep. The more I give to thee
The more I have, for both are infinite.
Romeo and Juliet, II i

A friend should bear his friend's infirmities.
Julius Caesar, IV ii

Poor naked wretches, wheresoe'er you are,
That bide the pelting of this pitiless storm,
How shall your houseless heads and unfed sides,
Your looped and windowed raggedness, defend you
From seasons such as these? O, I have ta'en
Too little care of this. Take physic, pomp,
Expose thyself to feel what wretches feel,
That thou mayst shake the superflux to them
And show the heavens more just.
King Lear, III iv

Good name in man and woman, dear my lord,
Is the immediate jewel of their souls.
Who steals my purse steals trash; 'tis something, nothing;
'Twas mine, 'tis his, and has been slave to thousands.
But he that filches from me my good name
Robs me of that which not enriches him
And makes me poor indeed.

Othello, III iii

Rightly to be great
Is not to stir without great argument,
But greatly to find quarrel in a straw
When honour's at the stake.

Hamlet, IV iv

We few, we happy few, we band of brothers.
For he today that sheds his blood with me
Shall be my brother; be he ne'er so vile,
This day shall gentle his condition.
And gentlemen in England now abed
Shall think themselves accursed they were not here,
And hold their manhoods cheap whiles any speaks
That fought with us upon St Crispin's day.

Henry V, IV iii

I love
The name of honour more than I fear death.

Julius Caesar, I ii

Once more unto the breach, dear friends, once more,
Or close the wall up with our English dead.
In peace there's nothing so becomes a man
As modest stillness and humility,
But when the blast of war blows in our ears,
Then imitate the action of the tiger.
Stiffen the sinews, conjure up the blood,
Disguise fair nature with hard-favoured rage.
Then lend the eye a terrible aspect,
Let it pry through the portage of the head
Like the brass cannon, let the brow o'erwhelm it
As fearfully as doth a gallèd rock
O'erhang and jutty his confounded base,
Swilled with the wild and wasteful ocean.
Now set the teeth and stretch the nostril wide,
Hold hard the breath, and bend up every spirit
To his full height. On, on, you noblest English,
Whose blood is fet from fathers of war-proof,
Fathers that like so many Alexanders
Have in these parts from morn till even fought,
And sheathed their swords for lack of argument.
Dishonour not your mothers; now attest
That those whom you called fathers did
   beget you.
Henry V, III i

True nobility is exempt from fear.
2 Henry VI, IV i

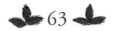

There is a tide in the affairs of men
Which, taken at the flood, leads on to fortune;
Omitted, all the voyage of their life
Is bound in shallows and in miseries.
On such a full sea are we now afloat,
And we must take the current when it serves,
Or lose our ventures.

Julius Caesar, IV ii

Perseverance, dear my lord,
Keeps honour bright. To have done is to hang
Quite out of fashion, like a rusty mail
In monumental mock'ry.

Troilus and Cressida, III iii

How poor are they that ha' not patience!
What wound did ever heal but by degrees?

Othello, II iii

Give me that man
That is not passion's slave, and I will wear him
In my heart's core, ay, in my heart of heart,
As I do thee.

Hamlet, III ii

The better part of valour is discretion.
1 Henry IV, V iv

He that can endure
To follow with allegiance a fall'n lord
Does conquer him that did his master
    conquer.
Antony and Cleopatra, III xiii

This Duncan
Hath borne his faculties so meek, hath been
So clear in his great office, that his virtues
Will plead like angels, trumpet-tongued against
The deep damnation of his taking-off.
Macbeth, I vii

I will a round unvarnished tale deliver.
Othello, I iii

There are no tricks in plain and simple faith.
Julius Caesar, IV ii

Simple truth miscalled simplicity.
Sonnet 66

O, then we bring forth weeds
When our quick winds lie still.
Antony and Cleopatra, I ii

O, beware, my lord, of jealousy.
It is the green-eyed monster which doth mock
The meat it feeds on.
Othello, III iii

Rumour is a pipe
Blown by surmises, Jealousy's conjectures...
2 Henry IV, Induction

But 'tis a common proof
That lowliness is young ambition's ladder,
Whereto the climber-upward turns his face;
But when he once attains the upmost round,
He then unto the ladder turns his back,
Looks in the clouds, scorning the base degrees
By which he did ascend.
Julius Caesar, II i

Yon Cassius has a lean and hungry look.
He thinks too much. Such men are dangerous.
Julius Caesar, I ii

Cromwell, I charge thee, fling away ambition.
By that sin fell the angels.
Henry VIII, III ii

Everything includes itself in power,
Power into will, will into appetite;
And appetite, an universal wolf. . .
Must make perforce an universal prey,
And last eat up himself.
Troilus and Cressida, I iii

Through tattered clothes great vices do appear;
Robes and furred gowns hide all. Plate sin with gold,
And the strong lance of justice hurtless breaks;
Arm it in rags, a pigmy's straw does pierce it.
King Lear, IV v

See how yon justice rails upon yon simple thief. . .
change places, and handy-dandy, which is the justice,
which is the thief.
King Lear, IV vi

O, it is excellent
To have a giant's strength, but it is tyrannous
To use it like a giant.
Measure for Measure, II ii

They are as sick that surfeit with too much
as they that starve with nothing.
Merchant of Venice, I ii

Like an eagle in a dove-cote. . .
Coriolanus, V vi

Is this a dagger which I see before me,
The handle toward my hand?

Macbeth, II i

Between the acting of a dreadful thing
And the first motion, all the interim is
Like a phantasma or a hideous dream.
The genius and the mortal instruments
Are then in counsel, and the state of man,
Like to a little kingdom, suffers then
The nature of an insurrection.

Julius Caesar, II i

The colour of the King doth come and go
Between his purpose and his conscience,
Like heralds 'twixt two dreadful battles set.
His passion is so ripe it needs must break.

King John, IV ii

 68

To hell, allegiance! Vows to the blackest devil!
Conscience and grace to the profoundest pit!
I dare damnation.

Hamlet, IV v

Why, I can smile, and murder whiles I smile,
And cry "Content!" to that which grieves my heart,
And wet my cheeks with artificial tears,
And frame my face to all occasions.

3 Henry VI, III ii

Unsex me here,
And fill me from the crown to the toe top-full
Of direst cruelty.

Macbeth, I v

Savage, extreme, rude, cruel, not to trust.

Sonnet 129

I am one, my liege,
Whom the vile blows and buffets of the world
Hath so incensed that I am reckless what
I do to spite the world.

Macbeth, III i

But man, proud man,
Dressed in a little brief authority...
...like an angry ape
Plays such fantastic tricks before high heaven
As makes the angels weep.

Measure for Measure, II ii

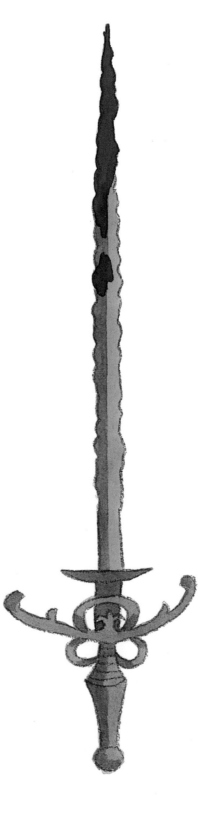

Get thee glass eyes,
And, like a scurvy politician, seem
To see the things thou dost not.
King Lear, IV v

Look like the innocent flower,
But be the serpent under't.
Macbeth, I v

A goodly apple rotten at the heart.
O, what a goodly outside falsehood hath!
The Merchant of Venice, I iii

...Oaths are straws, men's faiths are
wafer-cakes,
And Holdfast is the only dog, my duck.
Henry V, II iii

The devil can cite Scripture for his purpose.
The Merchant of Venice, I iii

...Breaking his oath and resolution like
A twist of rotten silk.
Coriolanus, V vi

The hearts
That spanieled me at heels, to whom I gave
Their wishes, do discandy, melt their sweets
On blossoming Caesar; and this pine is barked,
That overtopped them all.
Antony and Cleopatra, IV xiii

Oftentimes to win us to our harm
The instruments of darkness tell us truths,
Win us with honest trifles to betray's
In deepest consequence.
Macbeth, I iii

Has friendship such a faint and milky heart
It turns in less than two nights?
Timon of Athens, III i

Friendship is constant in all other things
Save in the office and affairs of love.
Therefore all hearts in love use their own tongues.
Let every eye negotiate for itself,
And trust no agent; for beauty is a witch
Against whose charms faith melteth into blood.
Much Ado About Nothing, II i

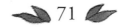

Look as I blow this feather from my face,
And as the air blows it to me again,
Obeying with my wind when I do blow,
And yielding to another when it blows,
Commanded always by the greater gust —
Such is the lightness of you common men.

3 Henry VI, III i

Our slippery people,
Whose love is never linked to the deserver
Till his deserts are passed.

Antony and Cleopatra, I ii

It hath been taught us from the primal state
That he which is was wished until he were,
And the ebbed man, ne'er loved till ne'er worth love,
Comes deared by being lacked. This common body,
Like to a vagabond flag upon the stream,
Goes to, and back, lackeying the varying tide,
To rot itself with motion.

Antony and Cleopatra, I iv

They'll take suggestion as a cat laps milk.

The Tempest, II i

I hate ingratitude more in a man
Than lying, vainness, babbling drunkenness,
Or any taint of vice whose strong corruption
Inhabits our frail blood.
Twelfth Night, III iv

Blow, winds, and crack your cheeks! Rage, blow,
You cataracts and hurricanoes, spout
Till you have drenched our steeples, drowned the cocks!
You sulph'rous and thought-executing fires,
Vaunt-couriers of oak-cleaving thunderbolts,
Singe my white head; and thou all-shaking thunder,
Strike flat the thick rotundity o'th' world,
Crack nature's moulds, all germens spill at once
That makes ingrateful man.
King Lear, III ii

How sharper than a serpent's tooth it is
To have a thankless child.
King Lear, I iv

All the stored vengeances of heaven fall
On her ingrateful top! Strike her young bones,
You taking airs, with lameness!...
You nimble lightnings, dart your blinding flames
Into her scornful eyes. Infect her beauty,
You fen-sucked fogs drawn by the pow'rful sun
To fall and blister.

King Lear, II ii

Now does he feel
His secret murders sticking on his hands.
Macbeth, V ii

Will all great Neptune's ocean wash this blood
Clean from my hand? No, this my hand will rather
The multitudinous seas incarnadine,
Making the green one red.
Macbeth, II ii

Here's the smell of the blood still. All the perfumes
of Arabia will not sweeten this little hand. O, O, O!
Macbeth, V i

And thus the whirligig of time brings in his revenges.
Twelfth Night, V i

Bow, stubborn knees; and heart with strings of steel,
Be soft as sinews of the new-born babe.
All may be well.
Hamlet, III iii

O sovereign mistress of true melancholy...
                                    Throw my heart
Against the flint and hardness of my fault.
Antony and Cleopatra, IV x

The rarer action is
In virtue than in vengeance. They being penitent,
The sole drift of my purpose doth extend
Not a frown further. Go release them, Ariel.
The Tempest, V i

The quality of mercy is not strained.
It droppeth as the gentle rain from heaven
Upon the place beneath. It is twice blest:
It blesseth him that gives, and him that takes.
The Merchant of Venice, IV i

No ceremony that to great ones 'longs,
Not the king's crown, nor the deputed sword,
The marshal's truncheon, nor the judge's robe,
Become them with one half so good a grace
As mercy does.
Measure for Measure, II ii

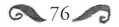

This is the excellent foppery of the world: that when we are sick in fortune —
often the surfeits of our own behaviour — we make guilty of our disasters the
sun, the moon, and stars, as if we were villains on necessity, fools by heavenly
compulsion, knaves, thieves, and treachers by spherical predominance,
drunkards, liars, and adulterers by an enforced obedience of planetary influence,
and all that we are evil in by a divine thrusting on.

King Lear, I ii

The fault, dear Brutus, is not in our stars,
But in ourselves, that we are underlings.

Julius Caesar, I ii

Use every man after his desert, and who
should 'scape whipping?

Hamlet, II ii

How would you be
If He which is the top of judgement should
But judge you as you are?

Measure for Measure, II ii

If there be
Yet left in heaven as small a drop of pity
As a wren's eye...

Cymbeline, IV ii

So our virtues
Lie in th'interpretation of the time.
Coriolanus, IV vii

Pray you now, forget
And forgive.
King Lear, IV vi

A peace above all earthly dignities,
A still and quiet conscience.
Henry VIII, III ii

So shines a good deed in a naughty world.
The Merchant of Venice, V i

OUR REVELS NOW ARE ENDED

Like as the waves make towards the pebbled shore,
So do our minutes hasten to their end,
Each changing place with that which goes before;
In sequent toil all forwards do contend.
Nativity, once in the main of light,
Crawls to maturity, wherewith being crowned
Crookèd eclipses 'gainst his glory fight,
And time that gave, doth now his gift confound.
Time doth transfix the flourish set on youth,
And delves the parallels in beauty's brow;
Feeds on the rarities of nature's truth,
And nothing stands but for his scythe to mow:
    And yet to times in hope my verse shall stand,
    Praising thy worth despite his cruel hand.

Sonnet 60

Let's do it after the high Roman fashion,
And make death proud to take us.
Antony and Cleopatra, IV xvi

If I must die,
I will encounter darkness as a bride,
And hug it in mine arms.
Measure for Measure, III i

Give me my Romeo, and when I shall die
Take him and cut him out in little stars,
And he will make the face of heaven so fine
That all the world will be in love with night
And pay no worship to the garish sun.
Romeo and Juliet, III ii

Death lies on her like an untimely frost
Upon the sweetest flower of all the field.
Romeo and Juliet, IV iv

Death, that hath sucked the honey of thy breath,
Hath had no power yet upon thy beauty.
Thou art not conquered. Beauty's ensign yet
Is crimson in thy lips and in thy cheeks,
And death's pale flag is not advancèd there.
Romeo and Juliet, V iii

         Eyes, look your last.
Arms, take your last embrace, and lips, O you
The doors of breath, seal with a righteous kiss
A dateless bargain to engrossing death.
Romeo and Juliet, V iii

The bright day is done,
And we are for the dark.

Antony and Cleopatra, V ii

O, withered is the garland of the war.
The soldier's pole is fall'n. Young boys and girls
Are level now with men. The odds is gone,
And there is nothing left remarkable
Beneath the visiting moon.

Antony and Cleopatra, IV xvi

Howl, howl, howl, howl! O, you are men of stones.
Had I your tongues and eyes, I'd use them so
That heaven's vault should crack. She's gone for ever.
I know when one is dead and when one lives.
She's dead as earth. Lend me a looking-glass.
If that her breath will mist or stain the stone,
Why, then she lives...
This feather stirs. She lives. If it be so,
It is a chance which does redeem all sorrows
That ever I have felt.

King Lear, V iii

My particular grief
Is of so floodgate and o'erbearing nature
That it engluts and swallows other sorrows,
And it is still itself.

Othello, I iii

Here is my journey's end, here is my butt
And very sea-mark of my utmost sail.

Othello, V ii

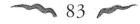

Fear no more the heat o'th' sun,
　　Nor the furious winter's rages.
Thou thy worldly task hast done,
　　Home art gone, and ta'en thy wages.
Golden lads and girls all must,
As chimney-sweepers, come to dust.

Fear no more the frown o'th' great,
　　Thou art past the tyrant's stroke.
Care no more to clothe and eat,
　　To thee the reed is as the oak.
The sceptre, learning, physic, must
All follow this, and come to dust.

Fear no more the lightning flash,
　　Nor th'all-dreaded thunder-stone.
Fear not slander, censure rash.
　　Thou hast finished joy and moan.
All lovers young, all lovers must
Consign to thee, and come to dust.
　　No exorciser harm thee,
　　Nor no witchcraft charm thee.
　　Ghost unlaid forbear thee.
　　Nothing ill come near thee.
　　Quiet consummation have,
　　And renownèd be thy grave!

Cymbeline, IV ii

Cowards die many times before their deaths;
The valiant never taste of death but once.
Of all the wonders that I yet have heard,
It seems to me most strange that men should fear,
Seeing that death, a necessary end,
Will come when it will come.

Julius Caesar, II ii

There's a divinity that shapes our ends,
Rough-hew them how we will.

Hamlet, V ii

Men must endure
Their going hence even as their coming hither.
Ripeness is all.

King Lear, V ii

Thou hast nor youth nor age,
But as it were an after-dinner's sleep
Dreaming on both.

Measure for Measure, III i

Full fathom five thy father lies.
   Of his bones are coral made;
Those are pearls that were his eyes;
   Nothing of him that doth fade
But doth suffer a sea-change
Into something rich and strange.
Sea-nymphs hourly ring his knell:
   Hark, now I hear them.
   Ding-dong bell.

The Tempest, I ii

God give them wisdom that have it; and those that are fools,
let them use their talents.

Twelfth Night, I v

FESTE

Good madonna, why mournest thou?

OLIVIA

Good fool, for my brother's death.

FESTE

I think his soul is in hell, madonna.

OLIVIA

I know his soul is in heaven, fool.

FESTE

The more fool, madonna, to mourn for
your brother's soul, being in heaven.

Twelfth Night, I v

I had rather have a fool to make me merry
than experience to make me sad.

As You Like It, IV i

The man that hath no music in himself,
Nor is not moved with concord of sweet sounds,
Is fit for treasons, stratagems, and spoils.
The Merchant of Venice, V i

In sweet music is such art,
Killing care and grief of heart.
Henry VIII, III i

The poet's eye, in a fine frenzy rolling,
Doth glance from heaven to earth, from earth to heaven,
And as imagination bodies forth
The forms of things unknown, the poet's pen
Turns them to shapes, and gives to airy nothing
A local habitation and a name.
A Midsummer Night's Dream, V i

Think, when we talk of horses, that you see them,
Printing their proud hoofs i'th' receiving earth;
For 'tis your thoughts that now must deck our kings,
Carry them here and there, jumping o'er times,
Turning th'accomplishment of many years
Into an hourglass.
Henry V, Prologue to Act I

...To hold as 'twere the mirror up to nature.
Hamlet, III ii

All the world's a stage,
And all the men and women merely players.
They have their exits and their entrances,
And one man in his time plays many parts,
His acts being seven ages. At first the infant,
Mewling and puking in the nurse's arms.
Then the whining schoolboy, with his satchel,
And shining morning face, creeping like snail
Unwillingly to school. And then the lover,
Sighing like furnace, with a woeful ballad
Made to his mistress' eyebrow. Then, a soldier,
Full of strange oaths, and bearded like the pard,
Jealous in honour, sudden, and quick in quarrel,
Seeking the bubble reputation
Even in the cannon's mouth. And then the justice,
In fair round belly with good capon lined,
With eyes severe and beard of formal cut,
Full of wise saws and modern instances;
And so he plays his part. The sixth age shifts
Into the lean and slippered pantaloon,
With spectacles on nose and pouch on side,
His youthful hose, well saved, a world too wide
For his shrunk shank, and his big, manly voice,
Turning again toward childish treble, pipes
And whistles in his sound. Last scene of all,
That ends this strange, eventful history,
Is second childishness and mere oblivion,
Sans teeth, sans eyes, sans taste, sans everything.

As You Like It, II vii

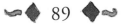

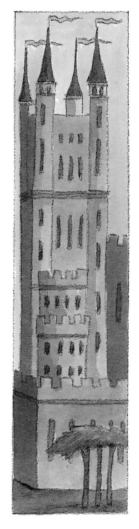

Our revels now are ended. These our actors,
As I foretold you, were all spirits, and
Are melted into air, into thin air:
And like the baseless fabric of this vision,
The cloud-capped towers, the gorgeous palaces,
The solemn temples, the great globe itself,
Yea, all which it inherit, shall dissolve;
And, like this insubstantial pageant faded,
Leave not a rack behind. We are such stuff
As dreams are made on, and our little life
Is rounded with a sleep.
The Tempest, IV i

A great while ago the world begun,
    With hey ho, the wind and the rain,
But that's all one, our play is done,
    And we'll strive to please you every day.
Twelfth Night, V i

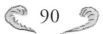

William Shakespeare

William Shakespeare was the son of John Shakespeare, a glove-maker and wool dealer, and Mary Arden, the daughter of a well-to-do farmer. He was born in Stratford-upon-Avon in Warwickshire and baptized there on April 26, 1564. He married Anne Hathaway in 1582 and in the next few years they had three children.

Shakespeare moved to London in about 1587. For the next twenty-five years he lived and worked in London, though he always maintained his links with Stratford. Shakespeare worked as an actor and a playwright, and was also busy in the management of the acting companies he belonged to. Eventually he became a permanent and leading member of a great acting company called The King's Men.

Shakespeare returned to live in Stratford in about 1610, and continued to write, at least until 1613. He died on April 23, 1616, aged fifty-two, and in 1623 a monument was erected to him in Holy Trinity Church. Shortly afterwards, two of his friends and colleagues from the King's Men published his collected plays in an edition that became known as the First Folio.

✦ SHAKESPEARE'S PLAYS AND POETRY ✦

Numbers refer to pages on which the plays or poems have been quoted.